LESSONS FROM GRIMM:
How to Write a Fairy Tale
Workbook

Shonna Slayton

AMARETTO PRESS

Cover design © Seedlings Design Studio
Interior design © SaRose Design

Paperback ISBN: 978-1-947736-05-4

Amaretto Press
Phoenix, AZ

Other Books by Shonna Slayton

Nonfiction

Lessons From Grimm: How To Write a Fairy Tale

Lessons From Grimm: How to Write a Fairy Tale (workbook series)

Writing Prompts From Grimm: A fairy-tale themed workbook for Grades 3-6

Writing Prompts From Grimm: A fairy-tale themed workbook for Grades 7-12

Fiction

Fairy-tale Inheritance Series

Cinderella's Dress

Cinderella's Shoes

Cinderella's Legacy

Snow White's Mirror

Beauty's Rose

The Little Mermaid (coming soon)

Lost Fairy Tales Series

The Tower Princess

Historical Women

Liz and Nellie: Nellie Bly and Elizabeth Bisland's Race Around the World in Eighty Days

Table of Contents

Introduction

THE PATTERN

When Grimms' fairy tales are boiled down to their simplest components, we have a pattern. This workbook uses that pattern to walk you through writing a fairy tale:

» <u>Once upon a time</u>
» there was a <u>character</u>
» who lived in a <u>setting</u>
» and had a <u>problem</u> (plot).
» Fairy tale <u>magic</u> intervened/interfered
» and everyone learned a <u>lesson</u> (theme).

HOW TO USE THIS WORKBOOK

This workbook is a companion workbook to *Lessons from Grimm: How to Write a Fairy Tale*. While not required to use this workbook, it is highly recommended.

SECTION 1: FIND YOUR FAIRY TALE VOICE

We're going to start building your fairy tale voice by pinpointing all the components you enjoy the most about fairy tales. In this first section, you'll analyze your favorite sub-genres, characters, settings, plots, and themes.

Here, you'll compile your personal lists of archetypes and tropes. Highlight what catches your attention in the samples and add your own favorites into the spaces provided. You can find the complete lists in the appendix section of *Lessons from Grimm*.

SECTION 2: BRAINSTORM YOUR FAIRY TALE

You'll be using this space to make notes about your fairy tale. You'll be given space to work out your chosen sub-genre, characters, settings, plots, themes, and fairy tale magic.

Exercise questions pulled from *Lessons from Grimm: How to Write a Fairy Tale* will help you think more deeply about each component.

SECTION 3 AND 4: BRAINSTORM MORE FAIRY TALES

These sections are a repeat of Section 2. In total, you could brainstorm three separate tales, or you could use the space to create a trilogy.

SECTION 1: FIND YOUR FAIRY TALE VOICE

ONCE UPON A TIME....*GENRE*

The first place we can choose our favorite fairy tale tropes and archetypes is in the sub-genres of the fairy tales themselves. Grimm's fairy tales cross many genres, from horror to romance. I've made a list of twelve based on common elements.

1. Royalty Tales (princesses)

2. Fables (talking animals)

3. Pourquoi Tales (origin stories)

4. Horror (suspense and blood)

5. Home Life (family relationships)

6. Fantasy (magic and dragons)

7. Humor (situational; reversals)

8. Magical Realism (real life with glimpses of magic)

9. Religious (God, Death, St. Peter, and allegory)

10. Military (discharged soldiers)

11. Romance (marriage and forgotten love)

12. Traveler Tales (setting out to seek one's fortune)

What genres do you enjoy reading? You can start with the above twelve categories and then expand from there. For example, you might enjoy reading historical romance fairy tales.

For each: What tropes are common to these genres? List as many as you can think of. *Lessons from Grimm* includes three or more from each sub-genre as well as additional romance tropes and horror examples in the appendix.)

Do some research to find "comp" titles. These are books that are similar to the one you're thinking about writing. Find at least three. It's okay if they're not exactly the same, but look for similarity in subject matter, tone, target readership.

1.

2.

3.

There was a ... *Character*

Go through this sampling of characters pulled from Grimms' stories and circle/highlight the ones that stand out to you. Then, add your own favorites. Use the space to expand the descriptions to include your favorite traits, descriptions, names, etc. Remember, you're building your fairy tale voice. How you handle character is one element of your voice.

Characters

apprentice
artisan, astronomer
beautiful, haughty princess
beggar
broom-maker
brothers
burgomaster
chamber maid
charcoal-burner
child's nurse
coachman
cook
court-shoemaker
cup-bearer
daughter of an innkeeper
daughter, never laughed
discharged soldier
drummer
faithful servant
ferryman
fiddler
fisherman
foster father
gardener
godfather

godmother
goldsmith
goose girl
helpful maiden
huntsman
hussar
innkeeper
jam seller
judge
king
king's armor-bearer
king's council
knight
locksmith
lord
magician
maid
merchant
miller's wife
musician
orphan
overly confident prince
page
peasant
poor farmer
poor man and woman

poor tailor
poor woodcutter
prince
princess
queen
robber
sentry
servant
shapeshifter thief
stepmother who is a witch
stepsister
swineherd's daughter
tailor
thief
trusted servants
waiting-maid
watchman by the gates
widow
wood cutter

Fairy Tale Characters

bird that grants wishes
changeling
Death
dragon
dwarfs/mannikins
elves

fox with nine tails
frog that prophesies
giants
gold chickens
golden bird
griffin
imp
lion who always tells the
truth
nixie
thumbling
unicorn
wise woman (fairy godmother)

People Enchanted and Turned Into

ant
bear
bull
cat
church
chandelier
cow
donkey
dove
dragon
duck
eagle
fish
fishpond
flower
fox
frog
half hedgehog

hen
lake
lion
nightingale
old man
poodle
raven
red stone landmark
rooster
rose-tree
rose
sea-hare
stag
stone
swan
toad
tree
whale
white horse
wood

Positive Traits

beautiful
compassionate
courageous
curious
fair of face
faithful
fearless
good and honorable
good heart
handsome
honest
joyous

kind
merry
old
pious and good
poor
silly
strong
wise
young

Negative Traits

bad heart
black of heart
crafty
cunning
deceitful
drunken
envious heart
evil-hearted
faithless
false
greedy
hard-hearted
haughty
hearts of stone
idle
liar
mocking
negligent
proud
stubborn
thief
vile
wicked

Add your own characters and traits:

Who lived in a ... *SETTING*

Go through this list of settings found in Grimms' fairy tales and highlight the ones that interest you:

Settings	Types of Trees	Timing
ballroom	apple tree	at midnight
bedroom	aspen tree	daybreak
bridge	fir tree	full moon
carriage	hazel bush	middle of winter
castle	hollow tree	six o'clock
cottage in the woods,	juniper tree	sunrise
forest	oak	two o'clock
fork in the road	old lime tree	three days
glass mountain	pear tree	seven days
hut in the forest	rose-tree,	seven years
inn	trees of gold, silver, and dia-	
kitchen	monds	
lake	tree with a door	
meadow		
mill		
murderer's den		
pasture		
pigeon house		
ravine		
river/river bank		
road		
robber's den		
sea		
stable		
tower		
town hung with black crape		
waste place		
well: portal to another world		

Add your own settings:

AND HAD A PROBLEM ... *PLOT*

Go through this list of plots found in Grimms' fairy tales and highlight the ones that interest you:

» after long wishing and praying for a child, one is born
» animals reveal the antagonist
» antagonist dresses in disguise as a peddler-woman
» arrested protagonist is given a chance to redeem himself by going to another kingdom to steal something from there
» assumptions lead to misunderstandings
» break the rule and be kicked out of paradise
» brother avenges brothers who have been swindled
» brother kills brother to claim the reward
» brothers steal what youngest brother obtained and act like they did the work
» challenge to find the lost gold crown, missing since ancient times
» contest to claim an inheritance
» contest to marry a princess
» deathbed promises
» eating the forbidden fruit/food/opening the forbidden door brings severe consequences
» faced with poverty and hunger, brothers set off into the world to seek their fortune
» faithful servant sacrifices himself to save the king
» false queen: murder the queen and put an imposter in her place, magically transformed but for one telltale sign that must be hidden
» find a lost object
» hide out in the woods while their lives are in danger
» king has a feast, inviting all the bachelors in the country in order to find a husband for the princess
» king manipulates his children but they thwart him in the end
» king tracks down his wife who had been sent into hiding after word came that he (falsely) wanted her killed
» lovers are separated, injured, yet find one another again

- » make a rash vow of revenge only to reverse it and protect the one you vowed to kill
- » man risks death to try to answer riddle and marry the princess
- » naive traveler gets swindled at an inn
- » old woman gives an invisibility cloak
- » pass a series of tests to get something from the king
- » plot a kidnapping
- » prince or princess travels to a distant kingdom
- » princess chooses to live as a commoner instead of marry someone she doesn't want to marry
- » princess disguises herself as kitchen maid.
- » princess forced to marry an evil man in order to bring peace
- » princess gives suitors sleeping draughts so they can't learn her secrets
- » princess is blackmailed against speaking the truth
- » queen hears someone crying and upon learning (falsely) the reason, sees opportunity and brings her home to meet her son
- » riddle to be solved
- » rival kills the rescuer while he sleeps
- » royalty pretending to be working class
- » see what is behind a locked door and life is changed
- » servant is suspected of stealing when he is innocent and sets out to prove it
- » servant sent in place of the royal
- » servant tries to cover up their own misdeed by lying to the other
- » shunned wise woman curses a baby in order to hurt the parents
- » someone is recognized because of a ring
- » stepmother relentlessly hunts down stepchild(ren) to kill them
- » suitors put to death if they fail the test
- » talking animals are often enchanted people
- » three sons compete for the kingdom by bringing home a series of "the most beautiful _____"
- » three tasks to break an enchantment are inscribed on stone table
- » three wishes gone wrong
- » true bride has to prove who she is
- » true bridegroom sneaks back into town the day before the wedding and sets up in the inn

- » use an invisibility cloak to learn a secret
- » victim of rumors
- » warned not to eat or drink, travelers take the advice and someone else gets poisoned
- » while a queen sleeps, her baby is stolen and she is blamed for it
- » widower marries a woman who has ulterior motives
- » wise women bestow gifts on a baby
- » youngest daughter accepts marriage proposal from unpopular man who later comes back a fine man

Add your own favorite plot tropes:

Magic intervenes/interferes

Go through this list of magic found in Grimms' fairy tales and highlight the ones that interest you:

- » backpack contains whatever is wished for inside
- » ball of yarn will unroll to reveal a hidden path
- » bone carved into a horn sings the song of the person's murder
- » cabbage that when eaten turns the person into a donkey; another cabbage turns them back into a human
- » dwarf ring that allows you to control air spirits
- » fiddle that draws people close or makes them dance
- » gold bird: feathers made of gold, eggs of solid gold
- » gold horse - runs faster than the wind
- » handkerchief with three drops of mother's blood gives princess protection
- » healing apples
- » healing leaves
- » healing water
- » horn: blows down all the walls and fortifications
- » invisibility cloak
- » leaves restore life
- » looking-glass which speaks the truth
- » needle that can sew anything together seamlessly
- » purse that never runs out of money
- » ring that gives wearer strength
- » sleeping potion
- » telescope that can see everything in heaven and earth
- » tree of golden fruit that only allows its owner to pick it
- » walnuts that hold beautiful dresses
- » wand to open doors
- » wand turns people into objects, stone
- » well that turns everything that touches its water to gold
- » wishing saddle, boots, cap, cloak or ring will take you where you wish to be
- » wishing table or wishing cloth covers itself with food when you command it

Add your own fairy tale magic:

And Everyone Learned . . . *Theme*

Go through this list of themes found in Grimms' fairy tales and highlight the ones that interest you:

GENERAL THEME . . . . SPECIFIC THEME

anger.. misplaced anger leads to foolish action

appearances.............................. do not judge others on their appearances

assumptions.............................. assumptions lead to misunderstandings

bravery.. don't sit idly by when you can stop a menace

commitment .... stay true and you'll be rewarded in the end

confidence .... boldness will be rewarded

courage....................................... try even though others have failed

deception................................... deception leads to downfall

deception................................... don't try to be someone you're not

envy.. envy leads to hatred

envy.. envy makes a person miserable

faith .... having faith will allow you to complete any task

family .... sisters can be relied upon to keep the family together

family .... the greatest reward is having a family

fear... fear is best met with bravery and courage

gratitude.................................... you appreciate what you had when it's gone

greed .... greed leads to dishonest behavior

helping others .... protect the innocent

honor .... the honorable will be restored

humility .... acting with humility gains respect

humility .... embrace humility and you can make the world better

integrity .... doing what you say you will do brings honor

jealousy .... jealousy becomes all-consuming

justice... people get their just reward in the end

kindness..................................... be kind to people and animals alike

love.. love is patient and waits

love.. love is worth fighting for

love .... love seeks the good for others
love .... true loves will find each other after a separation
loyalty .... stay true and you'll be rewarded
magic .... can be used for good or evil
motherly love .... a mother protects her children
perseverance .... be patient in affliction; things will get better
perseverance .... never give up on your goal
power .... ultimate power corrupts
pride .... a proud spirit will be humbled
pride .... boasting leads to trouble
pride .... pride leads to destruction
repentance .... repentance brings restoration
respect .... treat others with respect
safety .... beware of someone who is too controlling
trust .... trust but verify
truth .... truth wins in the end
wisdom .... don't make a contract without first knowing all the details
work ethic .... diligent work is rewarded

Add Your Own Themes

HOW TO STAND OUT: A TOUCH OF WHIMSY

What makes a fairy tale feel like a fairy tale? Often a touch of whimsy is found in the use of fairy tale magic, but it can also be in other areas. Think in terms of genre, setting, character, plot, and theme. Make notes here about your favorite whimsical fairy tale examples. (Grimm examples: a woman with a large thumb, a mountain made of glass, or a challenge to pluck a feather off a griffin.)

SECTION 2: BRAINSTORM YOUR OWN FAIRY TALE

GENRE

Now that you've thought about all the things you love in a fairy tale, start brainstorming your own story. Choose your favorite genre tropes (romance, magical realism, etc.) to include in your story. How can you connect these genre tropes in with popular fairy tale tropes? Brainstorm some ideas. (Examples: Romance tied with True Bride trope; magical realism tied with a magical object.)

CHARACTER OUTLINES:

Protagonist

Start with an archetype (princess in a tower, unloved stepchild, youngest prince), then build a full-fledged character.

Name:

Archetype:

Stakes:

Goal:

Motivation:

Need:

Conflict:

Personal History:

Strong emotions associated with the character:

Physical Characteristics:

Other Notes

1.   What have you done in your story to create empathy for your character? Be specific.

2.   What is virtuous about your main character? What will create admiration in the reader?

3.   What does your protagonist want? Why does it matter? (stakes)

4.   Why can't they have what they want right now? (conflict)

5.   List three potential strengths and three potential weaknesses for your protagonist.

6.   Are your character's motivations coming through in their actions and inner dialogue? Focus specifically on key turning points and make sure those moments are clear.

Antagonist

Name:

Archetype:

Stakes:

Goal:

Motivation:

Need:

Conflict:

Personal History:

Strong emotions (heart):

Physical Characteristics:

Other Notes:

Questions to Consider:

1. How can you show us what your character wants? Be specific. (goal)

2. Why can't they have it right now? (conflict)

3. List two potential strengths and two potential weaknesses for your antagonist.

4. Bonus: What physical object can your antagonist be associated with? (Evil queen—poison apple, forest witch—gingerbread house, or an odd little man and a spinning wheel.)

Use this space to list your side characters and the ways they will influence the plot. Consider the role of fairy tale characters like Grimms' wise women (fairy godmothers) and mentors who give magical gifts. Here are some questions to get you thinking. Make notes on the following pages.

1.   List your side characters. For each of these characters, how will they affect the protagonist? The plot?

2.   What is their standout characteristic? What do they have in common with Grimms' depictions? What is different?

3.   Consider the scene where the side character performs his or her most important role. Make it memorable for them as it is their shining moment (for good or bad!)

Regarding helpers

1. Who can your protagonist go to for help?

2. Will this help come in the form of advice or objects (or both)?

3. List three pieces of advice your protagonist needs to hear from a side character.

4. List three potential objects (magical or otherwise) your character could use.

Regarding fairy godmothers

1. Will your story have a fairy godmother/wise woman?

2. If so, what is her role? For good or for ill?

3. Will the fairy godmother/wise woman have a prior connection to the protagonist? What about the antagonist?

4. What form will her magic take? Will she give advice? An object? Both?

5. Set boundaries. What can't your fairy godmother/wise woman do?

1. Define the family relationships in your fairy tale—how well does everyone get along? If the dynamics are complicated, draw a web connecting everyone and marking the type of relationship on the connecting line.

2. Who are allies and who are at odds with one another? Explain.

3. How can you sweeten one of the relationships? Write notes for that scene.

4. How can you sour one of the family relationships? Write notes for that scene.

SETTING

Review the six ways the Grimms use setting:

- » to highlight a character's needs, wants, and goals;
- » to create obstacles for the hero or the villain;
- » to create opportunities vital to the plot;
- » to set up reversals;
- » to create a cohesive beginning and ending story structure;
- » to create atmosphere or tone.

Make notes on your setting, using questions on the next pages.

General settings:

1.   List at least three elements of setting that are important to your fairy tale. Consider natural landscape, architecture, climate.

2.   For each of those elements, brainstorm a list of descriptive words you can use when your characters are moving in that setting. Think of it like creating a palette, much like an artist would for a painting. Employ all of your character's senses: sight, sound, hearing, taste, smell, intuition. Come up with some fairy-tale like descriptions, adding a touch of whimsy.

3.   Create a story board for your setting. Attach images, sketch important backgrounds, or draw a map. (page 42)

4.   How can you use your setting to create atmosphere in your story?

5.   Find three important moments in your story to add atmosphere to heighten the moment.

Mountains:

1.   Describe any mountains in your story. Are they simply a backdrop, or is there something unique about them?

2.   Who lives on the mountain?

3.   What obstacles will your characters face on the mountain?

4.   Is there anything inside your mountain?

5.   Do you have a scene that can take place in a valley—people coming together or being trapped?

Forest Dwellings:

1. Describe any forest dwellings in your story.

2. What is unique about this place?

3. Who lives in the dwelling?

4. How will your characters be tested here?

Trees:

1. What kinds of trees are in your fairy tale? Can the type of tree be like one mentioned in Grimm?

2. Is there anything magical about your trees?

3. Can any of your scenes take place under a tree?

Roads

1. Is there a road in your fairy tale? If so, who or what does your character meet along the way? Any magical creatures or talking animals?

2. What challenges must be overcome along the road?

3. What opportunities arise along the road? Any objects or knowledge that could be found and used later?

4. Is your character making a decision? Consider placing a fork in the road that coincides with their decision-making process.

5. How does your character change as they go down this path?

Wells:

1. Is your well a portal? If so, how does it work? Can anyone go through it?

2. Are there riches to be obtained from the well?

3. What does your character learn or discover at the well?

Castles:

1. What makes your castle a fairy tale castle?

2. Is anything or anyone enchanted in the castle? How?

3. What obstacles exist for the characters in and around the castle (environment or people)?

Towers:

1. How can you use a tower in your fairy tale?

2. Can characters come and go freely from this tower?

3. Is there a way for you to give a subtle reference to one of the Grimms' tower references in your own story?

Plot : The Fairy Tale Synopsis

Use this space to create a synopsis of your story.

Normal world:

Show protagonist confronting a problem in regular world.

The inciting incident:

Explain what starts the story rolling; what sets up some mystery and foreshadows the beginnings of conflict.

First plot point:

Point of no return; the main character cannot go back to the way things were, they have to keep going forward until things are resolved.

Rising stakes:

List some problems and questions that propel us to keep reading: How will they survive and attain their goal?

Midpoint:

What is the midpoint reversal or reveal?

Dark moment:

Describe how things have never been worse for the protagonist.

Second plot point:

This is the final "things set in motion" major plot point.

Climax and conclusion:

Describe how the loose ends are tied up.

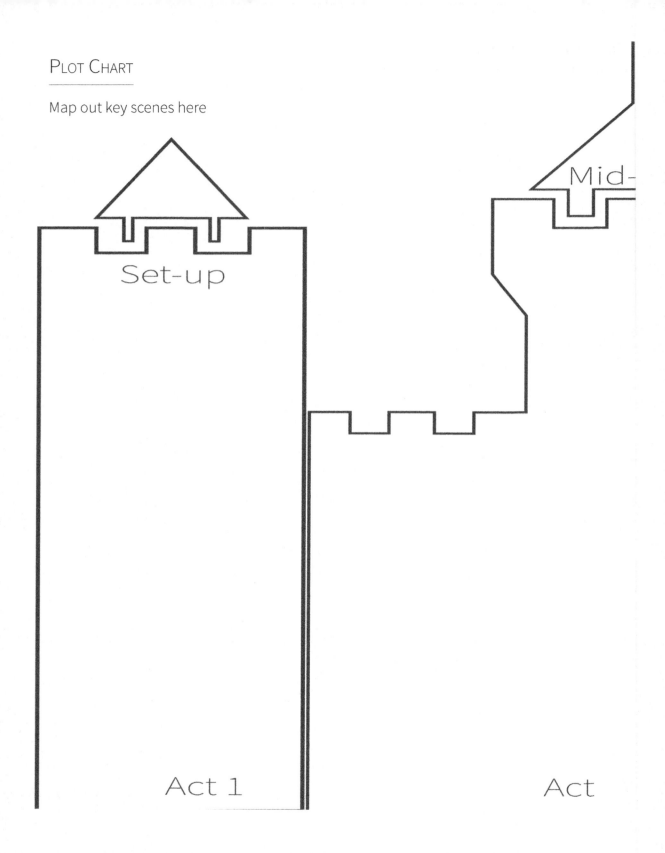

PLOT CHART

Map out key scenes here

Set-up

Mid-

Act 1

Act

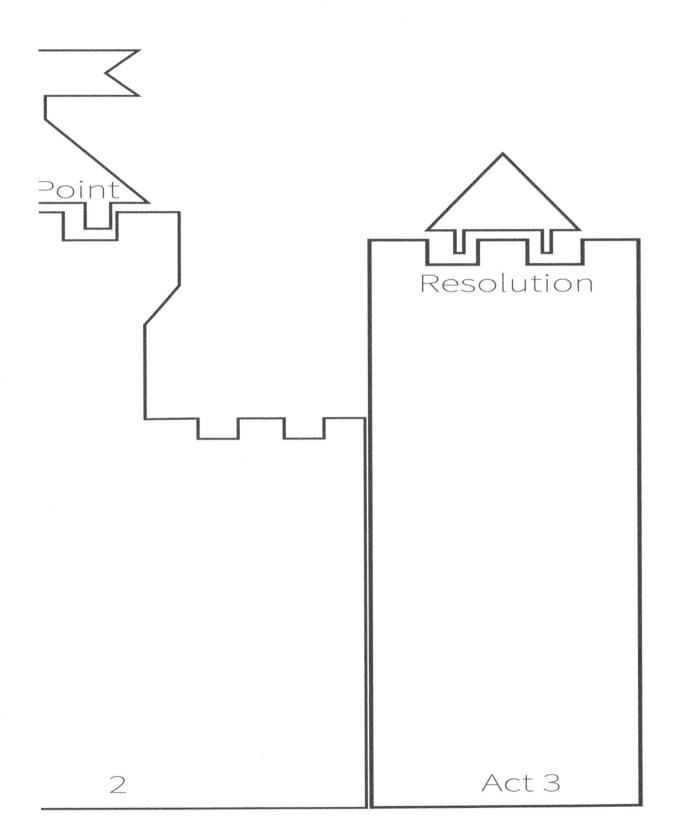

Romance Plot:

Romantic Settings

List potential locations; note specifics: sights, sounds, scents, etc.

Romantic characters

List potential dialogue; key phrases.

Romantic (Grand) Gesture

How will the character(s) prove their love?

First interaction:

Fun and games:

First realization/hint of feelings:

Break up:

Fighting for love:

Together at last:

Questions to consider:

1. Looking at your setting as a backdrop for a romantic plot, what specifically adds to the romance?

2. What is it about your characters' values that brings out the romance in them? What makes them worthy of each other? Use the plot to bring out these qualities in the characters. Don't be too subtle.

3. Which romance tropes relate the closest to your tale? What can you do to bring the trope out more?

4. Do you have a romantic grand gesture in the plot? A standout scene that will have readers talking about the story long after they read it?

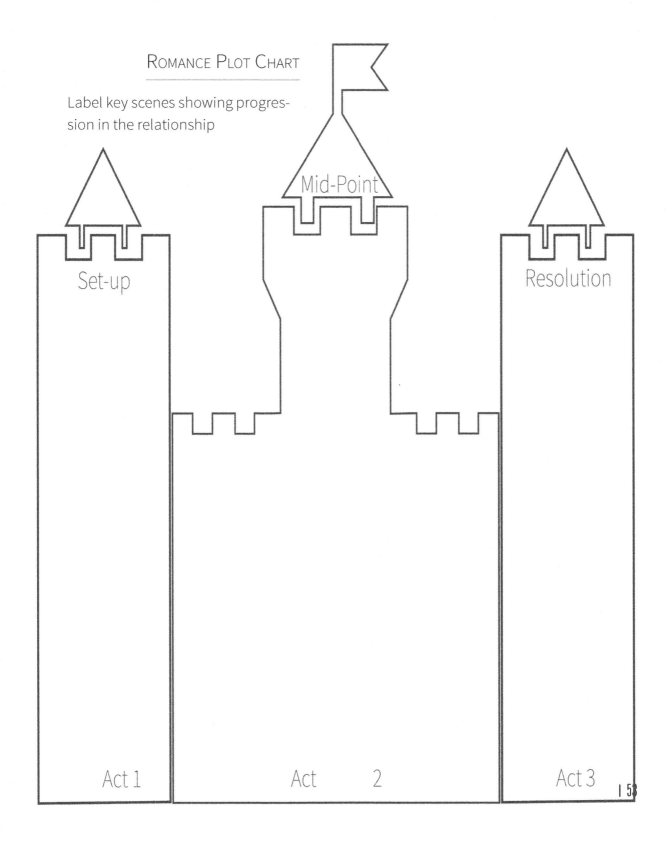

ROMANCE PLOT CHART

Label key scenes showing progression in the relationship

Mid-Point

Set-up

Resolution

Act 1

Act 2

Act 3

Plot Twists

For setting, character, and plot, write what you want readers to think, then the twist.

Setting:

Reader Expectations:

Twist:

Characters:

Reader Expectations:

Twist:

Plot:

Reader Expectations:

Twist:

Questions to Consider:

1. Is there a way for you to withhold information from the reader in a way that is organic (not forced or awkward) to the story?

2. How can you distract your readers while setting up the plot twist?

3. Do you have a character that you can disguise for a big reveal later? (at midpoint, or at the end?)

4. Why would the character want to be in disguise?

5. What prevents everyone from knowing who the character really is?

6. What are some creative ways to reveal the character's true identity?

Escalation: How to Make Things Worse

1.   Track where your fairy tale escalates the tension. Can you add more tension?

2.   Has the protagonist been confronted with an Impossible Bargain/Choice? Aside from escalating major plot points, what are some ways you can add micro-tension to escalate a scene?

3.   What is the communication like in the story? What happens when you change the plot by twisting a message?

Escalation Plot Chart

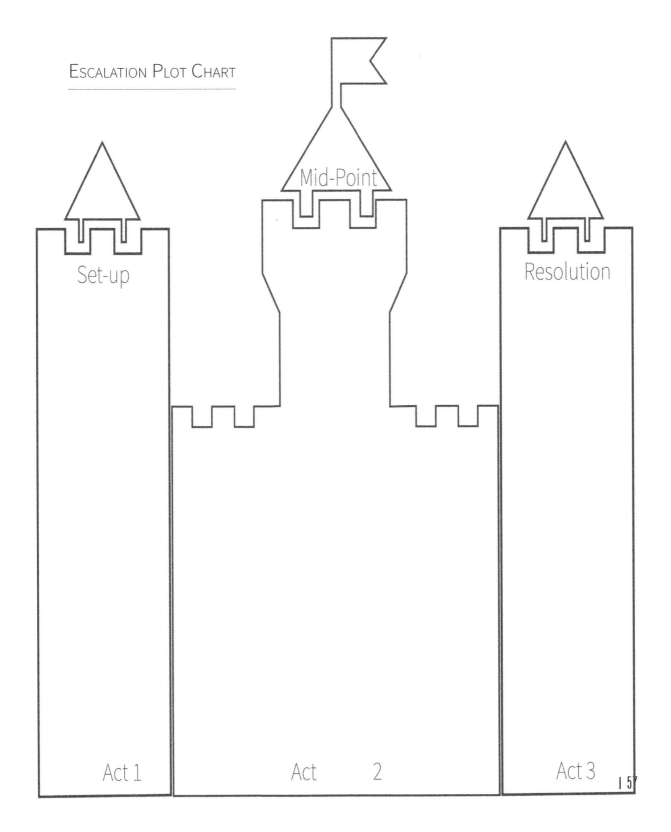

Mid-Point

Set-up

Resolution

Act 1

Act   2

Act 3

TEST OF THREE

What kind of tests are in your fairy tale? (Morality test, inheritance test, or marry-the-princess test?) In what ways can your character be tested three times? What is the reward for passing the test? List ways the protagonist is tested and the result.

1.

2.

3.

1.   Focus on your beginning and ending. Do you see the main story thread started in the beginning and wrapped up in the ending?

2.   How well does your beginning introduce the setting, the character, and the conflict?

3.   Do all the story threads get tied up in the end, or do they lead to a sequel? Even if a sequel is on the horizon, is the ending of this story satisfying enough for the reader?

FAIRY TALE MAGIC

You may have already brainstormed a lot of the magic when you looked at characters. Use this space to expand the magical worldbuilding.

1. Spend some time thinking about the fairy tale magic in your story. Does it line up with how magic is portrayed in Grimm or do you want it to explain more?

2. Who wields the fairy tale magic and how?

3. If you have a magical item, what happens when it falls into the wrong hands? Brainstorm several ideas.

4. How does the fairy tale magic relate to your protagonist? To the stakes in the plot?

5. Keeping the idea of transformation in mind, you can add another layer of depth to your story. How are your characters' inner selves changed by the magic they experience in the plot?

6. What is unique about your fairy tale magic? What is traditional about it?

Enchantments: Curses and Blessings

1.   List any enchantments in your fairy tale and map out where they are in the story. If you have a slow section, what would change if you added a new enchantment? A twist on the current enchantment?

2.   If your fairy tale contains a curse, examine how it works. Who gave it? Have you made the motivation clear, if not right away, by the end of the story?

3.   How is your curse broken?

4.   Does your fairy tale contain any blessings? Advice or magical items gifted by a wise woman or other fairy tale being? If not, consider adding one.

5.   How whimsical is your fairy tale magic? Is there a way for you to make it more so?

Magical Objects

1.   Take another look at any magical objects in your fairy tale and see if you can relate them to one of these in Grimm's tales. Observant fairy tale fans will notice the reference to these classic objects.

2.   We never see anyone making magical objects in Grimms' tales. Where do you think they come from?

3.   Consider using magical items as part of the setting and world building in your fairy tale, if not a necessary part of the plot.

Whimsy

Whimsy may seem like a small thing to consider when writing a fairy tale, but it's one of those elements that make a fairy tale a fairy tale. It's woven throughout all the other components.

Make a pass through everything you've brainstormed and find places where you can add whimsy. The Grimms often did this through humor and irony.

THEME

1. Examine possible themes in your own work. Do you have reoccurring themes that you keep going back to?

2. Do you use any motifs in your fairy tales? How often do they show up? Are they consistent in the meanings they imply?

3. Plan specific ways to strengthen the themes in your own fairy tales. Consider all the main sections we've looked at: genre, character, setting, plot, and fairy tale magic. How can they be used together to build toward one central theme?

Genre

Character

Setting

Plot

Fairy Tale Magic

FAITH AND FAIRY TALES

Use this space to outline your allegory or make notes on allusions or any spiritual awareness the characters have. If writing an allegory, note the deeper story underlying the tale and how it relates to the surface story.

SECTION 3: BRAINSTORM YOUR OWN FAIRY TALE

GENRE

Choose your favorite genre tropes (romance, magical realism, etc.) to include in your story. How can you connect these genre tropes in with popular fairy tale tropes? Brainstorm some ideas. (Examples: Romance tied with True Bride trope; magical realism tied with a magical object.)

CHARACTER OUTLINES:

Protagonist

Start with an archetype (princess in a tower, unloved stepchild, youngest prince), then build a full-fledged character.

Name:

Archetype:

Stakes:

Goal:

Motivation:

Need:

Conflict:

Personal History:

Strong emotions associated with the character:

Physical Characteristics:

Other Notes

1.   What have you done in your story to create empathy for your character? Be specific.

2.   What is virtuous about your main character? What will create admiration in the reader?

3.   What does your protagonist want? Why does it matter? (stakes)

4.   Why can't they have what they want right now? (conflict)

5.   List three potential strengths and three potential weaknesses for your protagonist.

6.   Are your character's motivations coming through in their actions and inner dialogue? Focus specifically on key turning points and make sure those moments are clear.

Antagonist

Name:

Archetype:

Stakes:

Goal:

Motivation:

Need:

Conflict:

Personal History:

Strong emotions (heart):

Physical Characteristics:

Other Notes:

Questions to Consider:

1. How can you show us what your character wants? Be specific. (goal)

2. Why can't they have it right now? (conflict)

3. List two potential strengths and two potential weaknesses for your antagonist.

4. Bonus: What physical object can your antagonist be associated with? (Evil queen—poison apple, forest witch—gingerbread house, or an odd little man and a spinning wheel.)

Side Characters

Use this space to list your side characters and the ways they will influence the plot. Consider the role of fairy tale characters like Grimms' wise women (fairy godmothers) and mentors who give magical gifts. Here are some questions to get you thinking. Make notes on the following pages.

1.   List your side characters. For each of these characters, how will they affect the protagonist? The plot?

2.   What is their standout characteristic? What do they have in common with Grimms' depictions? What is different?

3.   Consider the scene where the side character performs his or her most important role. Make it memorable for them as it is their shining moment (for good or bad!)

Regarding helpers

1. Who can your protagonist go to for help?

2. Will this help come in the form of advice or objects (or both)?

3. List three pieces of advice your protagonist needs to hear from a side character.

4. List three potential objects (magical or otherwise) your character could use.

Regarding fairy godmothers

1. Will your story have a fairy godmother/wise woman?

2. If so, what is her role? For good or for ill?

3. Will the fairy godmother/wise woman have a prior connection to the protagonist? What about the antagonist?

4. What form will her magic take? Will she give advice? An object? Both?

5. Set boundaries. What can't your fairy godmother/wise woman do?

1. Define the family relationships in your fairy tale—how well does everyone get along? If the dynamics are complicated, draw a web connecting everyone and marking the type of relationship on the connecting line.

2. Who are allies and who are at odds with one another? Explain.

3. How can you sweeten one of the relationships? Write notes for that scene.

4. How can you sour one of the family relationships? Write notes for that scene.

SETTING

Review the six ways the Grimms use setting:

- » to highlight a character's needs, wants, and goals;
- » to create obstacles for the hero or the villain;
- » to create opportunities vital to the plot;
- » to set up reversals;
- » to create a cohesive beginning and ending story structure;
- » to create atmosphere or tone.

Make notes on your setting, using questions on the next pages.

General settings:

1.   List at least three elements of setting that are important to your fairy tale. Consider natural landscape, architecture, climate.

2.   For each of those elements, brainstorm a list of descriptive words you can use when your characters are moving in that setting. Think of it like creating a palette, much like an artist would for a painting. Employ all of your character's senses: sight, sound, hearing, taste, smell, intuition. Come up with some fairy-tale like descriptions, adding a touch of whimsy.

3.   Create a story board for your setting. Attach images, sketch important backgrounds, or draw a map. (page 84)

4.   How can you use your setting to create atmosphere in your story?

5.   Find three important moments in your story to add atmosphere to heighten the moment.

Mountains:

1.   Describe any mountains in your story. Are they simply a backdrop, or is there something unique about them?

2.   Who lives on the mountain?

3.   What obstacles will your characters face on the mountain?

4.   Is there anything inside your mountain?

5.   Do you have a scene that can take place in a valley—people coming together or being trapped?

Forest Dwellings:

1. Describe any forest dwellings in your story.

2. What is unique about this place?

3. Who lives in the dwelling?

4. How will your characters be tested here?

Trees:

1. What kinds of trees are in your fairy tale? Can the type of tree be like one mentioned in Grimm?

2. Is there anything magical about your trees?

3. Can any of your scenes take place under a tree?

Roads

1. Is there a road in your fairy tale? If so, who or what does your character meet along the way? Any magical creatures or talking animals?

2. What challenges must be overcome along the road?

3. What opportunities arise along the road? Any objects or knowledge that could be found and used later?

4. Is your character making a decision? Consider placing a fork in the road that coincides with their decision-making process.

5. How does your character change as they go down this path?

Wells:

1. Is your well a portal? If so, how does it work? Can anyone go through it?

2. Are there riches to be obtained from the well?

3. What does your character learn or discover at the well?

Castles:

1.   What makes your castle a fairy tale castle?

2.   Is anything or anyone enchanted in the castle? How?

3.   What obstacles exist for the characters in and around the castle (environment or people)?

Towers:

1.   How can you use a tower in your fairy tale?

2.   Can characters come and go freely from this tower?

3.   Is there a way for you to give a subtle reference to one of the Grimms' tower references in your own story?

PLOT : THE FAIRY TALE SYNOPSIS

Use this space to create a synopsis of your story.

Normal world:
Show protagonist confronting a problem in regular world.

The inciting incident:
Explain what starts the story rolling; what sets up some mystery and foreshadows the beginnings of conflict.

First plot point:
Point of no return; the main character cannot go back to the way things were, they have to keep going forward until things are resolved.

Rising stakes:

List some problems and questions that propel us to keep reading: How will they survive and attain their goal?

Midpoint:

What is the midpoint reversal or reveal?

Dark moment:

Describe how things have never been worse for the protagonist.

Second plot point:

This is the final "things set in motion" major plot point.

Climax and conclusion:

Describe how the loose ends are tied up.

Map out key scenes here

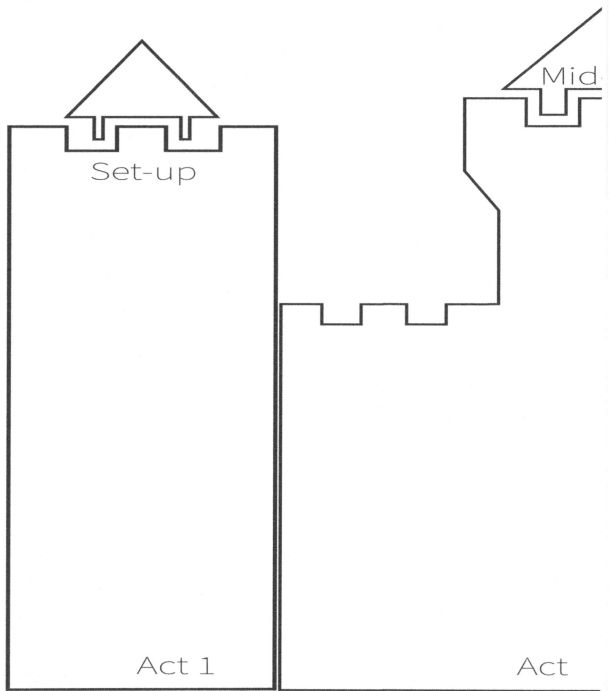

Set-up

Mid-

Act 1

Act

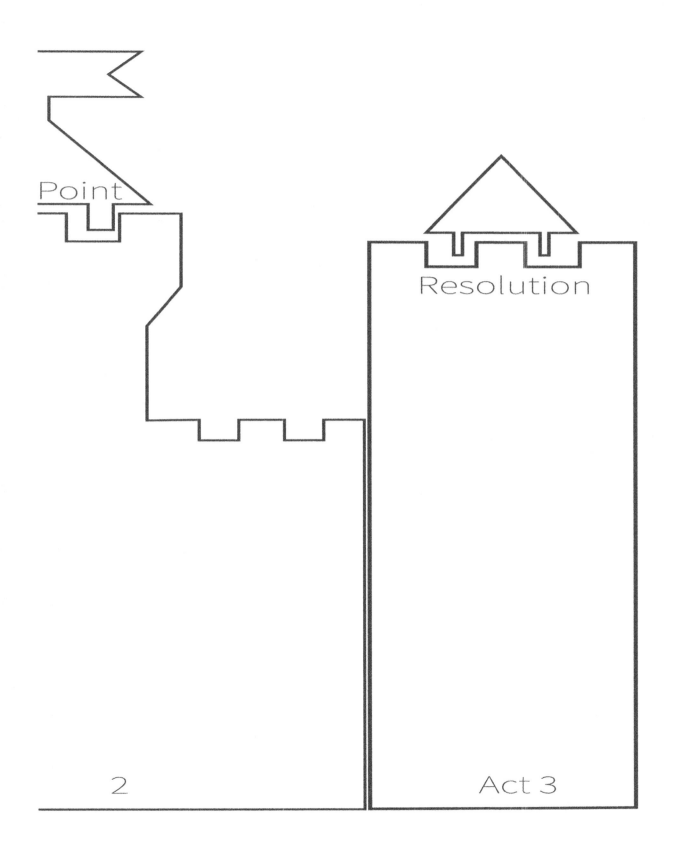

Point

Resolution

2

Act 3

Romantic Settings

List potential locations; note specifics: sights, sounds, scents, etc.

Romantic characters

List potential dialogue; key phrases.

Romantic (Grand) Gesture

How will the character(s) prove their love?

First interaction:

Fun and games:

First realization/hint of feelings:

Break up:

Fighting for love:

Together at last:

1.   Looking at your setting as a backdrop for a romantic plot, what specifically adds to the romance?

2.   What is it about your characters' values that brings out the romance in them? What makes them worthy of each other? Use the plot to bring out these qualities in the characters. Don't be too subtle.

3.   Which romance tropes relate the closest to your tale? What can you do to bring the trope out more?

4.   Do you have a romantic grand gesture in the plot? A standout scene that will have readers talking about the story long after they read it?

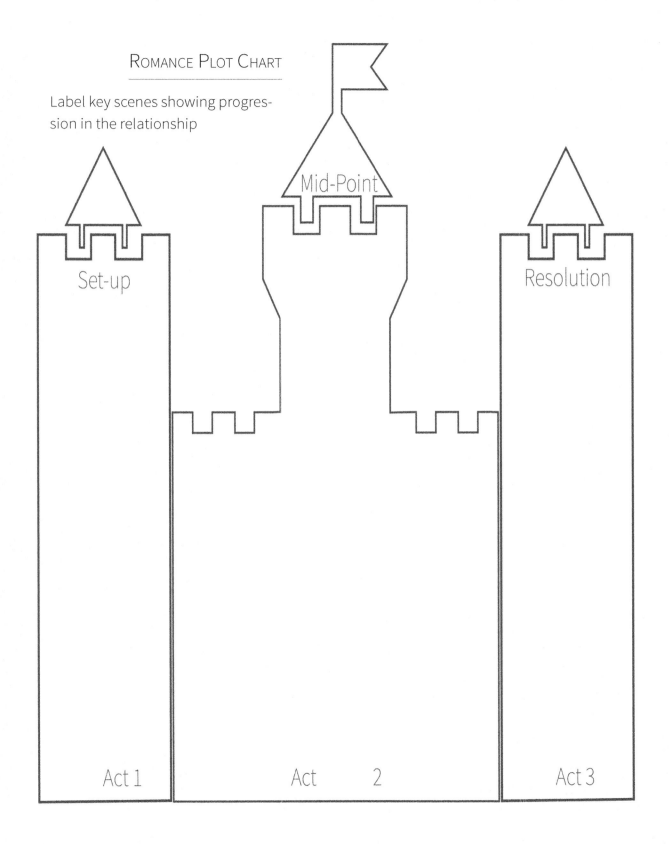

Plot Twists

For setting, character, and plot, write what you want readers to think, then the twist.

Setting:

Reader Expectations:

Twist:

Characters:

Reader Expectations:

Twist:

Plot:

Reader Expectations:

Twist:

Questions to Consider:

1. Is there a way for you to withhold information from the reader in a way that is organic (not forced or awkward) to the story?

2. How can you distract your readers while setting up the plot twist?

3. Do you have a character that you can disguise for a big reveal later? (at midpoint, or at the end?)

4. Why would the character want to be in disguise?

5. What prevents everyone from knowing who the character really is?

6. What are some creative ways to reveal the character's true identity?

ESCALATION: HOW TO MAKE THINGS WORSE

1.   Track where your fairy tale escalates the tension. Can you add more tension?

2.   Has the protagonist been confronted with an Impossible Bargain/Choice? Aside from escalating major plot points, what are some ways you can add micro-tension to escalate a scene?

3.   What is the communication like in the story? What happens when you change the plot by twisting a message?

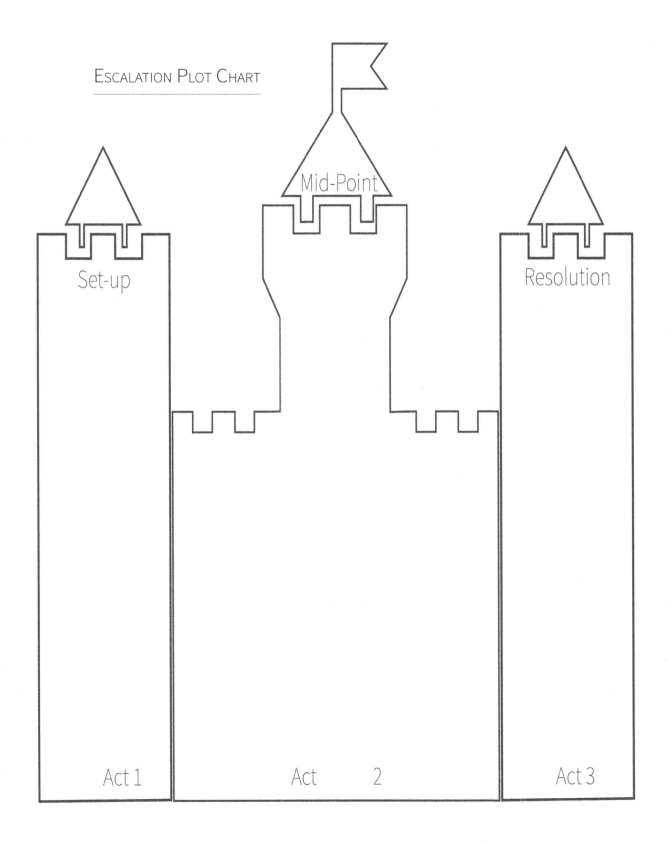

ESCALATION PLOT CHART

Mid-Point

Set-up

Resolution

Act 1

Act   2

Act 3

TEST OF THREE

What kind of tests are in your fairy tale? (Morality test, inheritance test, or marry-the-princess test?) In what ways can your character be tested three times? What is the reward for passing the test? List ways the protagonist is tested and the result.

1.

2.

3.

1.   Focus on your beginning and ending. Do you see the main story thread started in the beginning and wrapped up in the ending?

2.   How well does your beginning introduce the setting, the character, and the conflict?

3.   Do all the story threads get tied up in the end, or do they lead to a sequel? Even if a sequel is on the horizon, is the ending of this story satisfying enough for the reader?

FAIRY TALE MAGIC

You may have already brainstormed a lot of the magic when you looked at characters. Use this space to expand the magical worldbuilding.

1. Spend some time thinking about the fairy tale magic in your story. Does it line up with how magic is portrayed in Grimm or do you want it to explain more?

2. Who wields the fairy tale magic and how?

3. If you have a magical item, what happens when it falls into the wrong hands? Brainstorm several ideas.

4. How does the fairy tale magic relate to your protagonist? To the stakes in the plot?

5. Keeping the idea of transformation in mind, you can add another layer of depth to your story. How are your characters' inner selves changed by the magic they experience in the plot?

6. What is unique about your fairy tale magic? What is traditional about it?

Enchantments: Curses and Blessings

1.   List any enchantments in your fairy tale and map out where they are in the story. If you have a slow section, what would change if you added a new enchantment? A twist on the current enchantment?

2.   If your fairy tale contains a curse, examine how it works. Who gave it? Have you made the motivation clear, if not right away, by the end of the story?

3.   How is your curse broken?

4.   Does your fairy tale contain any blessings? Advice or magical items gifted by a wise woman or other fairy tale being? If not, consider adding one.

5.   How whimsical is your fairy tale magic? Is there a way for you to make it more so?

Magical Objects

1.   Take another look at any magical objects in your fairy tale and see if you can relate them to one of these in Grimm's tales. Observant fairy tale fans will notice the reference to these classic objects.

2.   We never see anyone making magical objects in Grimms' tales. Where do you think they come from?

3.   Consider using magical items as part of the setting and world building in your fairy tale, if not a necessary part of the plot.

WHIMSY

Whimsy may seem like a small thing to consider when writing a fairy tale, but it's one of those elements that make a fairy tale a fairy tale. It's woven throughout all the other components.

Make a pass through everything you've brainstormed and find places where you can add whimsy. The Grimms often did this through humor and irony.

Theme

1. Examine possible themes in your own work. Do you have reoccurring themes that you keep going back to?

2. Do you use any motifs in your fairy tales? How often do they show up? Are they consistent in the meanings they imply?

3. Plan specific ways to strengthen the themes in your own fairy tales. Consider all the main sections we've looked at: genre, character, setting, plot, and fairy tale magic. How can they be used together to build toward one central theme?

Genre

Character

Setting

Plot

Fairy Tale Magic

FAITH AND FAIRY TALES

Use this space to outline your allegory or make notes on allusions or any spiritual awareness the characters have. If writing an allegory, note the deeper story underlying the tale and how it relates to the surface story.

SECTION 4: BRAINSTORM YOUR OWN FAIRY TALE

GENRE

Choose your favorite genre tropes (romance, magical realism, etc.) to include in your story. How can you connect these genre tropes in with popular fairy tale tropes? Brainstorm some ideas. (Examples: Romance tied with True Bride trope; magical realism tied with a magical object.)

CHARACTER OUTLINES:

Protagonist

Start with an archetype (princess in a tower, unloved stepchild, youngest prince), then build a full-fledged character.

Name:

Archetype:

Stakes:

Goal:

Motivation:

Need:

Conflict:

Personal History:

Strong emotions associated with the character:

Physical Characteristics:

Other Notes

1. What have you done in your story to create empathy for your character? Be specific.

2. What is virtuous about your main character? What will create admiration in the reader?

3. What does your protagonist want? Why does it matter? (stakes)

4. Why can't they have what they want right now? (conflict)

5. List three potential strengths and three potential weaknesses for your protagonist.

6. Are your character's motivations coming through in their actions and inner dialogue? Focus specifically on key turning points and make sure those moments are clear.

Name:

Archetype:

Stakes:

Goal:

Motivation:

Need:

Conflict:

Personal History:

Strong emotions (heart):

Physical Characteristics:

Other Notes:

1. How can you show us what your character wants? Be specific. (goal)

2. Why can't they have it right now? (conflict)

3. List two potential strengths and two potential weaknesses for your antagonist.

4. Bonus: What physical object can your antagonist be associated with? (Evil queen—poison apple, forest witch—gingerbread house, or an odd little man and a spinning wheel.)

Side Characters

Use this space to list your side characters and the ways they will influence the plot. Consider the role of fairy tale characters like Grimms' wise women (fairy godmothers) and mentors who give magical gifts. Here are some questions to get you thinking. Make notes on the following pages.

1.   List your side characters. For each of these characters, how will they affect the protagonist? The plot?

2.   What is their standout characteristic? What do they have in common with Grimms' depictions? What is different?

3.   Consider the scene where the side character performs his or her most important role. Make it memorable for them as it is their shining moment (for good or bad!)

Regarding helpers

1. Who can your protagonist go to for help?

2. Will this help come in the form of advice or objects (or both)?

3. List three pieces of advice your protagonist needs to hear from a side character.

4. List three potential objects (magical or otherwise) your character could use.

Regarding fairy godmothers

1. Will your story have a fairy godmother/wise woman?

2. If so, what is her role? For good or for ill?

3. Will the fairy godmother/wise woman have a prior connection to the protagonist? What about the antagonist?

4. What form will her magic take? Will she give advice? An object? Both?

5. Set boundaries. What can't your fairy godmother/wise woman do?

1.   Define the family relationships in your fairy tale—how well does everyone get along? If the dynamics are complicated, draw a web connecting everyone and marking the type of relationship on the connecting line.

2.   Who are allies and who are at odds with one another? Explain.

3.   How can you sweeten one of the relationships? Write notes for that scene.

4.   How can you sour one of the family relationships? Write notes for that scene.

Setting

Review the six ways the Grimms use setting:

- » to highlight a character's needs, wants, and goals;
- » to create obstacles for the hero or the villain;
- » to create opportunities vital to the plot;
- » to set up reversals;
- » to create a cohesive beginning and ending story structure;
- » to create atmosphere or tone.

Make notes on your setting, using questions on the next pages.

1. List at least three elements of setting that are important to your fairy tale. Consider natural landscape, architecture, climate.

2. For each of those elements, brainstorm a list of descriptive words you can use when your characters are moving in that setting. Think of it like creating a palette, much like an artist would for a painting. Employ all of your character's senses: sight, sound, hearing, taste, smell, intuition. Come up with some fairy-tale like descriptions, adding a touch of whimsy.

3. Create a story board for your setting. Attach images, sketch important backgrounds, or draw a map. (page 126)

4. How can you use your setting to create atmosphere in your story?

5. Find three important moments in your story to add atmosphere to heighten the moment.

Mountains:

1. Describe any mountains in your story. Are they simply a backdrop, or is there something unique about them?

2. Who lives on the mountain?

3. What obstacles will your characters face on the mountain?

4. Is there anything inside your mountain?

5. Do you have a scene that can take place in a valley—people coming together or being trapped?

Forest Dwellings:

1. Describe any forest dwellings in your story.

2. What is unique about this place?

3. Who lives in the dwelling?

4. How will your characters be tested here?

Trees:

1. What kinds of trees are in your fairy tale? Can the type of tree be like one mentioned in Grimm?

2. Is there anything magical about your trees?

3. Can any of your scenes take place under a tree?

Roads

1. Is there a road in your fairy tale? If so, who or what does your character meet along the way? Any magical creatures or talking animals?

2. What challenges must be overcome along the road?

3. What opportunities arise along the road? Any objects or knowledge that could be found and used later?

4. Is your character making a decision? Consider placing a fork in the road that coincides with their decision-making process.

5. How does your character change as they go down this path?

Wells:

1. Is your well a portal? If so, how does it work? Can anyone go through it?

2. Are there riches to be obtained from the well?

3. What does your character learn or discover at the well?

Castles:

1. What makes your castle a fairy tale castle?

2. Is anything or anyone enchanted in the castle? How?

3. What obstacles exist for the characters in and around the castle (environment or people)?

Towers:

1. How can you use a tower in your fairy tale?

2. Can characters come and go freely from this tower?

3. Is there a way for you to give a subtle reference to one of the Grimms' tower references in your own story?

Plot : The Fairy Tale Synopsis

Use this space to create synopsis of your story.

Normal world:
Show protagonist confronting a problem in regular world.

The inciting incident:
Explain what starts the story rolling; what sets up some mystery and foreshadows the beginnings of conflict.

First plot point:
Point of no return; the main character cannot go back to the way things were, they have to keep going forward until things are resolved.

Rising stakes:

List some problems and questions that propel us to keep reading: How will they survive and attain their goal?

Midpoint:

What is the midpoint reversal or reveal?

Dark moment:

Describe how things have never been worse for the protagonist.

Second plot point:

This is the final "things set in motion" major plot point.

Climax and conclusion:

Describe how the loose ends are tied up.

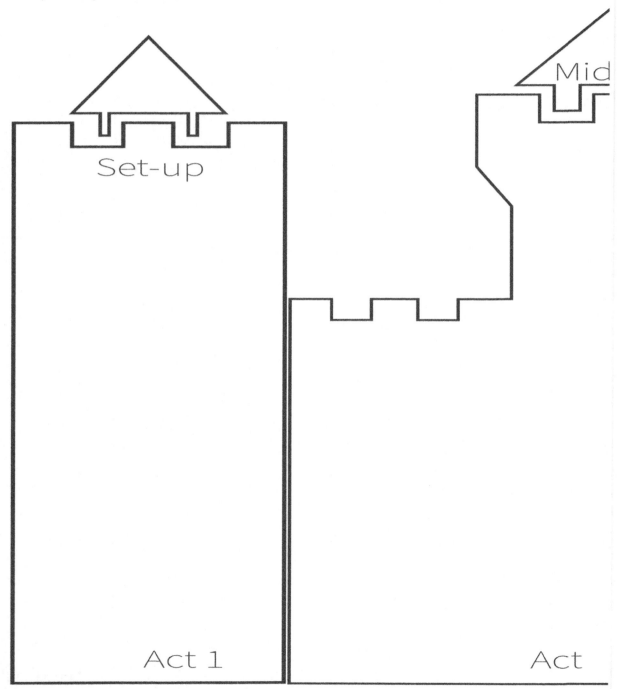

Set-up

Mid

Act 1

Act

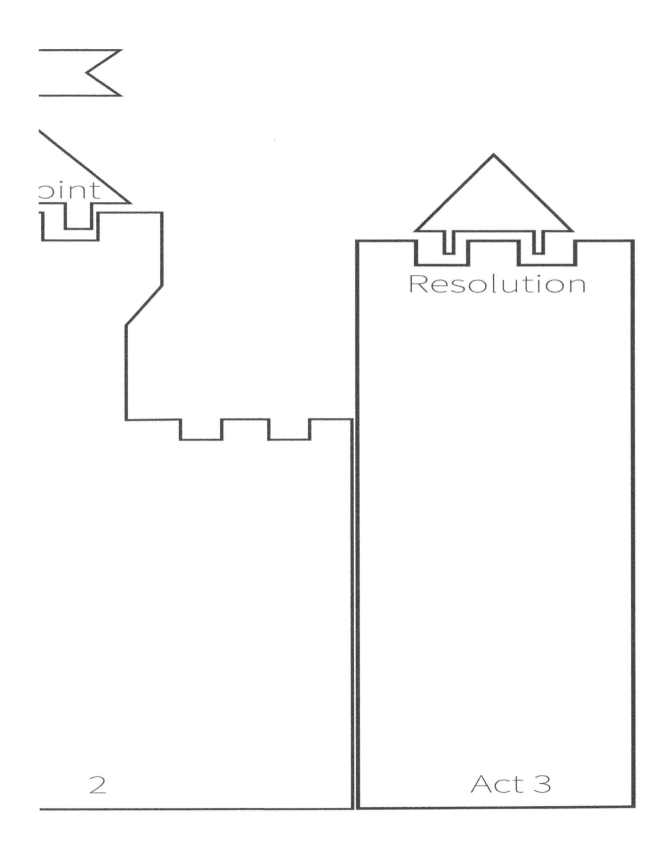

int

Resolution

2

Act 3

Romance Plot:

Romantic Settings
List potential locations; note specifics: sights, sounds, scents, etc.

Romantic characters
List potential dialogue; key phrases.

Romantic (Grand) Gesture
How will the character(s) prove their love?

First interaction:

Fun and games:

First realization/hint of feelings:

Break up:

Fighting for love:

Together at last:

1.   Looking at your setting as a backdrop for a romantic plot, what specifically adds to the romance?

2.   What is it about your characters' values that brings out the romance in them? What makes them worthy of each other? Use the plot to bring out these qualities in the characters. Don't be too subtle.

3.   Which romance tropes relate the closest to your tale? What can you do to bring the trope out more?

4.   Do you have a romantic grand gesture in the plot? A standout scene that will have readers talking about the story long after they read it?

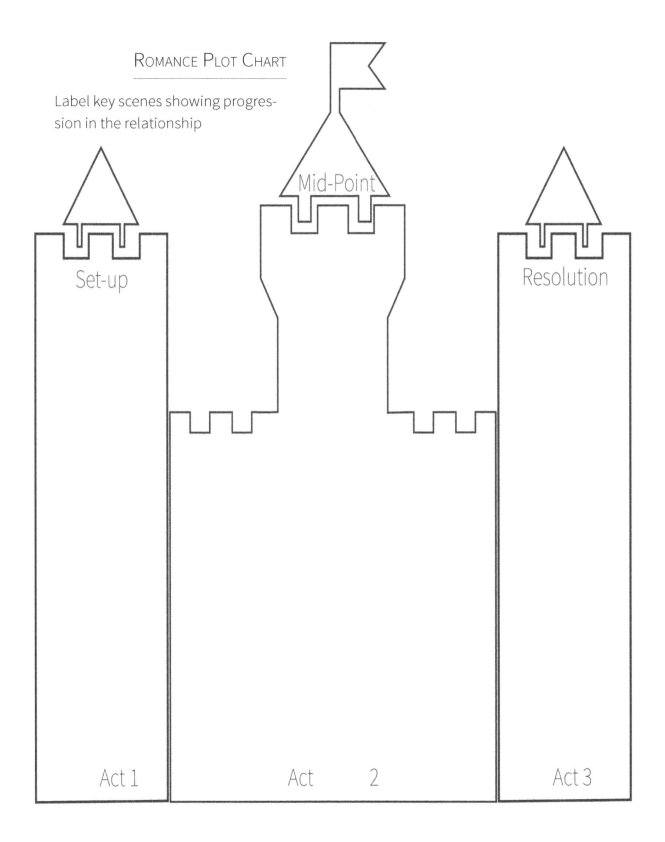

ROMANCE PLOT CHART

Label key scenes showing progression in the relationship

Mid-Point

Set-up

Resolution

Act 1

Act 2

Act 3

Plot Twists

For setting, character, and plot, write what you want readers to think, then the twist.

Setting:

Reader Expectations:

Twist:

Characters:

Reader Expectations:

Twist:

Plot:

Reader Expectations:

Twist:

Questions to Consider:

1. Is there a way for you to withhold information from the reader in a way that is organic (not forced or awkward) to the story?

2. How can you distract your readers while setting up the plot twist?

3. Do you have a character that you can disguise for a big reveal later? (at midpoint, or at the end?)

4. Why would the character want to be in disguise?

5. What prevents everyone from knowing who the character really is?

6. What are some creative ways to reveal the character's true identity?

ESCALATION: HOW TO MAKE THINGS WORSE

1. Track where your fairy tale escalates the tension. Can you add more tension?

2. Has the protagonist been confronted with an Impossible Bargain/Choice?

3. Aside from escalating major plot points, what are some ways you can add micro-tension to escalate a scene?

4. What is the communication like in the story? What happens when you change the plot by twisting a message?

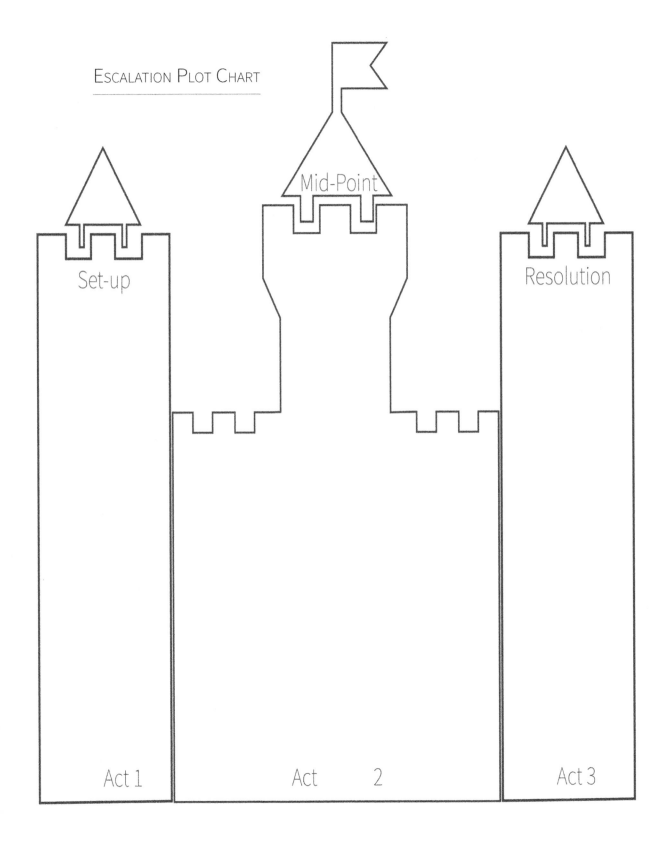

ESCALATION PLOT CHART

Mid-Point

Set-up

Resolution

Act 1

Act   2

Act 3

TEST OF THREE

What kind of tests are in your fairy tale? (Morality test, inheritance test, or marry-the-princess test?) In what ways can your character be tested three times? What is the reward for passing the test? List ways the protagonist is tested and the result.

1.

2.

3.

1.   Focus on your beginning and ending. Do you see the main story thread started in the beginning and wrapped up in the ending?

2.   How well does your beginning introduce the setting, the character, and the conflict?

3.   Do all the story threads get tied up in the end, or do they lead to a sequel? Even if a sequel is on the horizon, is the ending of this story satisfying enough for the reader?

Fairy Tale Magic

You may have already brainstormed a lot of the magic when you looked at characters. Use this space to expand the magical worldbuilding.

1. Spend some time thinking about the fairy tale magic in your story. Does it line up with how magic is portrayed in Grimm or do you want it to explain more?

2. Who wields the fairy tale magic and how?

3. If you have a magical item, what happens when it falls into the wrong hands? Brainstorm several ideas.

4. How does the fairy tale magic relate to your protagonist? To the stakes in the plot?

5. Keeping the idea of transformation in mind, you can add another layer of depth to your story. How are your characters' inner selves changed by the magic they experience in the plot?

6. What is unique about your fairy tale magic? What is traditional about it?

Enchantments: Curses and Blessings

1.   List any enchantments in your fairy tale and map out where they are in the story. If you have a slow section, what would change if you added a new enchantment? A twist on the current enchantment?

2.   If your fairy tale contains a curse, examine how it works. Who gave it? Have you made the motivation clear, if not right away, by the end of the story?

3.   How is your curse broken?

4.   Does your fairy tale contain any blessings? Advice or magical items gifted by a wise woman or other fairy tale being? If not, consider adding one.

5.   How whimsical is your fairy tale magic? Is there a way for you to make it more so?

Magical Objects

1.   Take another look at any magical objects in your fairy tale and see if you can relate them to one of these in Grimm's tales. Observant fairy tale fans will notice the reference to these classic objects.

2.   We never see anyone making magical objects in Grimms' tales. Where do you think they come from?

3.   Consider using magical items as part of the setting and world building in your fairy tale, if not a necessary part of the plot.

WHIMSY

Whimsy may seem like a small thing to consider when writing a fairy tale, but it's one of those elements that make a fairy tale a fairy tale. It's woven throughout all the other components.

Make a pass through everything you've brainstormed and find places where you can add whimsy. The Grimms often did this through humor and irony.

THEME

1.   Examine possible themes in your own work. Do you have reoccurring themes that you keep going back to?

2.   Do you use any motifs in your fairy tales? How often do they show up? Are they consistent in the meanings they imply?

3.   Plan specific ways to strengthen the themes in your own fairy tales. Consider all the main sections we've looked at: genre, character, setting, plot, and fairy tale magic. How can they be used together to build toward one central theme?

Genre

Character

Setting

Plot

Fairy Tale Magic

FAITH AND FAIRY TALES

Use this space to outline your allegory or make notes on allusions or any spiritual awareness the characters have. If writing an allegory, note the deeper story underlying the tale and how it relates to the surface story.

Fairy Tale Archetypes and Tropes

If you'd like a separate pdf of the appendix lists found in *Lessons from Grimm: How to Write a Fairy Tale*, go to:

ShonnaSlayton.com/GRIMMpdf/

Here, you can access the link to download Grimms' Fairy Tale Archetypes and Tropes. At the same time, you'll be added to my author newsletter so we can stay in touch.

Also by Shonna